A Sweet Singer

A Sweet Singer

Written by Marla Martin

Illustrated by Lois Myer and Marla Martin

This book may not be reproduced without written permision.

Rod and Staff Publishers, Inc.
P.O. Box 3, 14193 Hwy. 172
Crockett, Kentucky 41413
Telephone: (606) 522-4348

Printed in U.S.A.
Code no. 76-9-01
Catalog no. 2425

le

To-day was a day Lee would nev-er for-get. He did not know it, but to-day God had a sur-prise for him.

It was Sun-day and a very hot af-ter-noon. Lee walked to the back porch and looked for a cool spot. Then he spied the old wood-en chair. It was an old chair in-deed and had sat on the porch for many sum-mers. A thick, green vine curled above (ə-buv) it and made pleasant (plez-ənt) shade.

Lee tucked one foot un-der him and sat down. The old chair creaked and seemed al-most too big. But it was a good spot and a pleasant place to be on a hot af-ter-noon.

All was qui-et and very still. E-ven the birds seemed too hot to sing. Lee was hot, too, but not too hot to think.

Lee had a wish deep in his heart (härt). He thought (thôt) and thought a-bout that wish. He sat on the old wood-en chair and thought—

"I wish I had a friend (frend) to talk with to-day. But I am a-lone on the old wood-en chair. I am a-lone un-der the thick, green vine!"

Then a soft breeze blew. It fanned Lee's cheek and played with the leaves. Lee liked the breeze. He liked to feel it fan his cheek. He liked to watch it play with the leaves.

But the breeze was not the friend Lee wished for. He could not talk with the breeze, and the breeze could not talk to Lee.

Then Lee looked down. A little ant crawled o-ver his toes. It tick-led the humps and bumps of his toes. Lee wig-gled his toes and watched to see what the ant would do. Lee liked the ant. The ant was in-ter-est-ing to watch.

But the ant was not the friend Lee wished for. He could not talk with the little ant, and the little ant could not talk to Lee.

Then Lee looked up. He peeked be-tween the leaves of the thick, green vine. He saw the sky, big and blue. A white cloud-puff skipped far a-way. It looked like a wool-ly ram at play. Lee liked the cloud-puff and watched to see where it would go.

But the cloud-puff was not the friend Lee wished for. He could not talk with the cloud-puff, and the cloud-puff could not talk to Lee.

A little crick-et start-ed to sing. It sat on a long, wide leaf and sang. Lee turned to see. Its little wings rubbed o-ver its back. Fast-er and fast-er! Back and forth! Lee smiled as he watched. He liked the crick-et. He liked its song.

But the crick-et was not the friend Lee wished for. He could not talk with the little crick-et, and the little crick-et could not talk to Lee.

Lee was qui-et and very still as he sat on the old, wood-en chair. His tucked-under-foot went to sleep. But Lee was think-ing and did not mind. He thought and thought. He sat under the thick, green vine and thought—

"I like the crick-et.
I like the breeze,
The cloud-puff and ant.
I like all these.

"But they can-not hear,
Nor can they share

In my little joys
And child-ish care.

"I wish for a friend
On this hot day,
One that can hear and
Know what I say."

Lee thought of the wish that was
in his heart. And as he thought—

The soft, little breeze
Blew far away
To other children
At their play.

The little ant crawled
Home to its nest
Un-der the ground
To take a rest.

The white cloud-puff skipped
     Off like a ram
To a grass-y green
     Where played a lamb (lam).

The gay, little crick-et
Stopped its song,
Hopped un-der a leaf,
Wide and long.

Then all was qui-et and very still as Lee sat on the old wood-en chair. It was so very qui-et and so very still that Lee's eye-lids (ī-lids) drooped and then went shut. His head began to nod. Lee was a-sleep! He was a-sleep on the old wood-en chair un-der the thick, green vine.

One min-ute went by, then two and three. Lee slept on and all was still. Four min-utes went by, then five and six. Lee slept on and on. Sev-en min-utes went by, then eight and nine.

Hark!

Lee sat up straight (strāt). Both eyes o-pened wide! What had he heard?

Hark! There it was again (ə-gen) —so sweet and clear!

Lee rubbed his eyes. Was he dream-ing? But Lee was wide a-wake now. He was not dream-ing.

Again and again the song came. It fell sweet-ly on Lee's ear and made his eyes twin-kle like little stars.

The notes of the sweet sing-er danced (danst) up and down—up and down—up and down—up! The song tum-bled high into the air. Up and down—up and down—up and down—up!

What was the little bird try-ing to say? Were there words to fit with the song? Lee thought as he lis-tened. He would think of words.

Lee's eyes twin-kled bright-er as the song grew sweet-er. Then sud-den-ly words came. As the little bird sang, it seemed to say—

"Your Friend—your Friend—your Friend is God! Your Friend—your Friend—your Friend is God!"

The words fit per-fect-ly. Lee smiled as he lis-tened. He smiled and thought—

"I am not a-lone on the old wood-en chair. I am not a-lone un-der the thick, green vine."

Lee could hear the sweet sing-er, but he could not see it. Lee wanted very much to see the sweet sing-er. The little bird was high in a tree. It was hiding in the leaves. Lee could not climb (klīm) that high in a tree. He could not get close to the little bird.

Then Lee smiled. He sat on the old wood-en chair and smiled. He thought—

"God made the little bird. The lit-tle bird must do just what God tells it to do. God is my Friend. I will talk with my Friend."

Lee fold-ed his hands and whis-
pered soft-ly—

"Dear God, I want so much to see
The little bird up in the tree,
But it is hiding now from me.

"If it would please You, Father dear,
Tell that sweet bird to fly quite near
To me, as I am sit-ting here.

"I know You made the little bird.
And now I thank You that You heard
My sim-ple prayer (prâr), yes ev-ery
word!"

Lee sat on the old wood-en chair and waited. With twin-kling eyes he waited. Then sud-den-ly the little bird stopped sing-ing. It dived from the top of the tree down to a big grape-vine.

Lee held his breath (breth). There was the little bird! It was on the grape-vine right in front of him just six jumps away.

The little bird hopped from leaf to leaf. It seemed not to know just what to do. Then it hopped on a twig and started to sing—

"Your Friend—your Friend—your Friend is God!"

The plump, little bird could not keep still. Its tail stuck up in the air and flicked back and forth quick-ly. Its bright, brown feathers (feth-ərs) fluttered. When it cocked its head from side to side, Lee saw a white stripe over its eye.

Lee looked and looked at the pretty white stripe. He looked and looked at the little bird. And as he looked, the little bird sud-den-ly zoomed away. It zoomed away like a little jet!

Lee caught (côt) his breath. How could the little bird fly so fast?

Lee sat on the old wood-en chair and thought a-bout God. How kind God was to send the sweet bird!

Lee whis-pered with de-light to his Friend—

"Thank You for send-ing
    The sweet bird to me.
Thank You for bring-ing
    It down from the tree.

"And now I won-der,
    O Lord, how I do.
What fam-i-ly does
    This bird be-long to?

"Is it a wax-wing,
    A wren (ren) or a jay?
I'll look in my book
    Of birds right away."

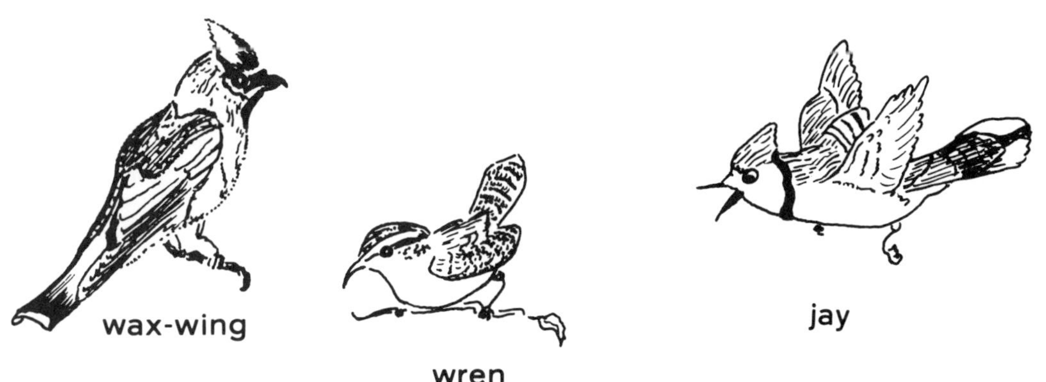

Then Lee went off for his bird book. He raced like the wind and was soon back on the old wood-en chair.

Lee looked and looked in the big bird book. He looked for a bird that was dressed just like the sweet sing-er. Then what did he see? On the wren page, he saw three birds that looked just like the sweet sing-er!

Each bird had a white stripe o-ver its eye. Each bird was dressed in bright, brown feathers. Lee knew then that the sweet sing-er was a wren. But he did not know which kind of wren.

Lee wished he could re-mem-ber bet-ter just how the little bird looked. If only the little bird would come back again. But the little bird had zoomed away, and Lee did not know where it went.

Then Lee whis-pered in his heart to God—

"Lord, if You wish,
Please send the little bird once (wuns) more
So that I can look and know for sure (shoor)
Which wren it is."

Then Lee wait-ed again. God had sent the little bird the first time. He could do it again. Lee wait-ed with the bird book o-pened wide on his lap. When the sweet sing-er came, he would look close-ly to see which wren it was.

One min-ute went by. Lee looked at the hills far a-way.

Two min-utes went by. Lee sniffed the air of a hot sum-mer day.

Three min-utes went by—and then, the little wren came. It came soft-ly and qui-et-ly and sat on a wire very close to Lee.

Lee saw it plain-ly. He saw the white stripe o-ver its eye. He saw white dots on its brown wing and a white patch un-der its throat. He saw its gold breast (brest).

Lee looked at the wren and then at his book. He knew then what the name of the little wren was. It was Car-o-li-na wren.

Lee was de-light-ed! This was his first time to see a Car-o-li-na wren, and it was just three jumps away!

And then the little wren came clos-er! It flew to the thick, green vine o-ver the old wood-en chair and sat on a twig right o-ver Lee's head. Sweet-ly it sang its little song—

"Your Friend—your Friend—your Friend is God! Your Friend—your Friend—your Friend is God!"

Lee was so sur-prised and so ex-ci-ted that he felt like a tea-ket-tle when it bub-bles over. He bub-bled with joy as he whis-pered to God—

"Thank You for send-ing
The little wren.
Thank You for bring-ing
It back again!"

Hop! Hop! The little wren hopped to a new place on the thick, green vine.

Lee looked up at the sweet, little wren, and the sweet, little wren looked down at Lee. They looked and looked.

And then—the sweet, little wren flew away. It flew soft-ly and qui-et-ly on its way.

Lee smiled as he sat on the old wood-en chair. He smiled and thought—

"God sent a sur-prise
    To me to-day.
God is my Friend
    And hears what I say."

Lee thought and thought, and as
he thought—

The soft breeze came back
And fanned his face.
The ant came out
Of its rest-ing place.

The cloud skipped back like
A bird on wing.
The crick-et start-ed
To sing and sing.

But Lee did not see and feel or hear these things. His heart was sing-ing too loud a song. It sang as he sat on the old wood-en chair. It sang as he sat under the thick, green vine. It sang and sang this little song—

"Three things, O Lord,
   I learned to-day:
You always hear
   Me when I pray.
Your kind-ness, Lord,
   Knows not an end.
You are a child's
   Most lov-ing Friend!

"The little bird
    You sent so sweet,
Taught (tôt) me these things;
    Still I'll re-peat–
You are a child's
    Most lov-ing Friend;
Help me to love
    You to the end."

Pronunciation Key

Short Vowel Sounds

a   *a*t
e   y*e*s
i   b*i*g
o   G*o*d
u   *u*s

Long Vowel Sounds

ā   m*a*de
ē   h*e*
ī   l*i*ke
ō   n*o*
yōō   *u*se

Other Vowel Sounds

a   *a*ir, th*ere*
ä   f*a*ther
ô   *o*r, l*o*ng
û(r)   *u*rge, *ear*th
ə   *a*bout
oi   b*oy*, *oi*l
ou   *ou*t, n*ow*
o͞o   f*oo*d, y*ou*
o͝o   g*oo*d, f*u*ll

The th Sounds

th   *th*ings
th   *th*is